A Benjamin Blog
and his Inquisitive Dog
Guide

Germany

Anita Ganeri

heinemann
raintree

To contact Capstone Global Library please phone 800-747-4992, or visit our website
www.capstonepub.com

Edited by Helen Cox Cannons
Designed by Philippa Jenkins and Tim Bond
Original illustrations © Capstone Global Library Limited 2015
Original map illustration by Oxford Designers and Illustrators
Ben and Barko Illustrated by Sernur ISIK
Picture research by Svetlana Zhurkin
Production by Helen McCreath
Originated by Capstone Global Library Limited
Printed and bound in China by CTPS

19 18 17 16 15
10 9 8 7 6 5 4 3 2 1

Library of Congress Cataloging-in-Publication Data
Ganeri, Anita, 1961-
  Germany / Anita Ganeri.
     pages cm.—(Country guides, with Benjamin Blog and his inquisitive dog)
  Includes bibliographical references and index.
  ISBN 978-1-4109-7994-0 (hb)—ISBN 978-1-4109-8000-7 (pb)— ISBN 978-1-4109-8011-3 (ebook) 1.
Germany—Juvenile literature. I. Title.

DD17.G258 2015
943—dc23   2014043975

This book has been officially leveled by using the F&P Text Level Gradient™ Leveling System.

Acknowledgments
We would like to thank the following for permission to reproduce photographs: Alamy: Bildarchiv Monheim
GmbH, 6; Dreamstime: Kuan Leong Yong, 7, Victormro, cover; Getty Images: Ulrich Baumgarten, 15;
iStockphoto: rotofrank, 25, totalpics, 17; Newscom: ABACA/DPA/Jan Woitas, 24, picture alliance/Arco
Images/G. Schulz, 11, picture alliance/Chromorange/Alexander Bernhard, 16, Zuma Press/Hemis/John
Frumm, 23; Shutterstock: Brent Hofacker, 20, canadastock, 4, chbaum, 9, FamVeld, 14, flowgraph, 28, Jenny
Sturm, 27, ksl, 13, Laszlo Szirtesi, 22, Luciano Morpurgo, 10, Marcel Wenk, 8, Noppasin, 12, Olaf Schulz, 19,
Roberto Zocchi, 26, 29, Scirocco340, 18, YaiSirichai, 21.

Some words are shown in bold, **like this.** You can find
out what they mean by looking in the glossary.

007332CTPSF15

Contents

Welcome to Germany! 4

The Story of Germany 6

Mountains, Forests, and Rivers 8

Super Cities 12

Guten Morgen! 14

Feeling Hungry 20

Sports and Music. 22

From Fast Cars to Wind Farms. 24

And Finally... .26

Germany Fact File 28

Germany Quiz 29

Glossary *30*

Find Out More *31*

Index *32*

Welcome to Germany!

Hello! My name is Benjamin Blog, and this is Barko Polo, my **inquisitive** dog. (He's named after the ancient explorer **Marco Polo**.) We have just returned from our latest adventure—exploring Germany. We put this book together from some of the blog posts we wrote along the way.

Country borders

DENMARK

Baltic Sea

• Kiel

North Sea

• Hamburg

Elbe

THE
NETHERLANDS

• Bremen

Berlin ■

POLAND

Balver Höhle
•

G E R M A N Y

• Düsseldorf
• Cologne

BELGIUM

Rhine

• Frankfurt

Main

LUXEMBOURG

CZECH
REPUBLIC

FRANCE

N

Danube

• Munich

Lake Constance

▲ Zugspitze

SWITZERLAND

AUSTRIA

BARKO'S BLOG-TASTIC GERMANY FACTS

Germany is a large country in Europe. On land, it has borders with nine other countries—Denmark, the Netherlands, Belgium, Luxembourg, France, Switzerland, Austria, the Czech Republic, and Poland.

The Story of Germany

Posted by: Ben Blog | May 15 at 10:36 a.m.

We're starting our tour in Aachen, in the west of Germany. This was the capital city of **Emperor** Charlemagne (747–814 CE), one of the most important leaders in German history. He is buried in this magnificent gold-and-silver **casket** in Aachen Cathedral.

BARKO'S BLOG-TASTIC GERMANY FACTS

After World War II, Germany was split into two countries—West Germany and East Germany. The city of Berlin was also divided by a high concrete wall. In 1989, the Berlin Wall was pulled down, and Germany became one country again.

Mountains, Forests, and Rivers

Posted by: Ben Blog | June 19 at 12 p.m.

Next, we headed south to the Zugspitze in Bavaria, on the border between Germany and Austria. At 9,718 feet (2,962 meters), it is the highest mountain in Germany. Instead of climbing, we're taking the cable car up. I'm hoping to get a photo of the cross on the top.

BARKO'S BLOG-TASTIC GERMANY FACTS

The beautiful Black Forest in southwest Germany gets its name from its dark, **coniferous** trees. It is a great place to go hiking. The longest trail is around 174 miles (280 kilometers) long.

We're taking a boat trip along the Rhine River, which flows from Switzerland through Germany. I wanted to see the famous Lorelei rock. Legend says that it is home to a beautiful **maiden** with golden hair. You can hear her singing, if you listen carefully.

BARKO'S BLOG-TASTIC GERMANY FACTS

The Wadden Sea National Park is a huge stretch of marshes and **mudflats** along the German coast of the North Sea. It's a great spot for birdwatching—look at that Arctic tern!

Super Cities

Posted by: Ben Blog | July 31 at 6:12 p.m.

Welcome to Berlin, the capital city of Germany. It is famous for the Reichstag (**parliament** building), Tierpark (zoo), and Fernsehturm (television tower). This is the Brandenburg Gate. For years, no one was allowed through the gate, until the Berlin Wall fell in 1989.

BARKO'S BLOG-TASTIC GERMANY FACTS

Hamburg is the city with the second-biggest population in Germany. It lies on the Elbe River and is also the country's main **port**. Every year, in May, there is a party for the port's birthday!

TERMINAL BURCHARDKAI

TERMINAL BURCHARDKAI

TERMINAL BURCHARDKAI

TERMINAL BURCHARDKAI

HHLA

DORNBUSCH
HAMBURG

Guten Morgen!

Posted by: Ben Blog | August 30 at 3:18 p.m.

I've been trying to learn some German while we're here. *Guten Morgen* means "Good morning." *Auf Wiedersehen* means "Goodbye." If you know someone very well, you can say *Tschüss!* for goodbye instead. *Ich heisse Benjamin Blog* means "My name is Benjamin Blog."

BARKO'S BLOG-TASTIC GERMANY FACTS

Nearly 81 million people live in Germany. Most of them are Germans. There are also many people from countries such as Turkey and Italy who moved to Germany to find work.

German children start school when they are six years old. Their first day at school is marked by a special gift called a *Schultüte* (schoolbag). This is a big paper cone, decorated with pictures and stickers and filled with toys, candy, pens, pencils, and books.

BARKO'S BLOG-TASTIC GERMANY FACTS

Just under three-quarters of German people live in cities. City people live in apartments. This apartment building is built in the Altbau style, which means "Old Building."

It was time to do some Christmas shopping, so we headed to the amazing Christmas market in Nuremberg. There are 180 stalls there, decorated in red-and-white cloth. There are lots of yummy things to eat, including plum people and gingerbread men.

BARKO'S BLOG-TASTIC GERMANY FACTS

Many German people are Christians, and there are beautiful churches all over Germany. This is the magnificent Cologne Cathedral. Its spires are more than 515 feet (157 meters) tall.

19

Feeling Hungry

Posted by: Ben Blog | January 14 at 5:46 p.m.

Germany is famous for making *wurst* (that's German for sausage). There are over 150 kinds of *wurst*. I was hungry and decided to try some *bratwurst*. You can eat it on a bun and with *sauerkraut* (pickled cabbage), potato salad, or a dollop of mustard. Yum!

BARKO'S BLOG-TASTIC GERMANY FACTS

Schwarzwälder Kirschtorte (Black Forest gateau) is a delicious German cake. It is made from layers of chocolate cake, with whipped cream and cherries in between.

21

Sports and Music

Posted by: Ben Blog | February 1 at 3:32 p.m.

Our next stop was the Allianz Arena in Munich. Barko and I are here to watch a soccer game. This is the home field of Bayern Munich, one of the top teams in Germany. German people love soccer. Germany won the World Cup in Brazil in 2014.

BARKO'S BLOG-TASTIC GERMANY FACTS

The Berlin Philharmonic Orchestra is one of the leading orchestras in the world. It plays music by many famous German **composers**, including Beethoven, Bach, and Brahms.

From Fast Cars to Wind Farms

Posted by: Ben Blog | March 17 at 9:01 a.m.

Car making is one of Germany's main industries, and German factories make some of the world's fastest and best-quality cars. This factory in Leipzig produces around 500 Porsche cars every day. We're off to take a tour of the factory and see how they are made.

BARKO'S BLOG-TASTIC GERMANY FACTS

This huge wind farm in Emden, in northwest Germany, is one of the biggest in Europe. **Wind turbines** like these turn the power of the wind into electrical power.

And Finally...

Our trip is nearly over, but we have saved the best for last. Here is a photo that I took of Neuschwanstein Castle in Bavaria. It perches on a mountaintop and was built by King Ludwig II. Sleeping Beauty's castle at Disneyland is based on this fairy-tale place.

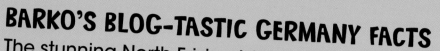

BARKO'S BLOG-TASTIC GERMANY FACTS

The stunning North Frisian Islands lie off the northwest coast of Germany. Sylt is the biggest island. It is joined to the mainland by a **causeway**, and you can take a train across.

I am here!

Germany Fact File

Area: 137,846 square miles
(357,022 square kilometers)

Population: 80,716,000 (2014)

Capital city: Berlin

Other main cities: Hamburg, Munich, Cologne,
Frankfurt am Main

Language: German

Main religion: Christianity

Highest mountain: Zugspitze (9,718 feet/
2,962 meters)

Longest river: Rhine
(537 miles/865 kilometers long in Germany)

Currency: Euro

Germany Quiz

Find out how much you know about Germany with our quick quiz.

1. Which German city was divided in two?
a) Munich
b) Berlin
c) Cologne

2. What does *auf Wiedersehen* mean?
a) Goodbye
b) Good morning
c) How are you?

3. What is *bratwurst*?
a) a type of sausage
b) a type of salad
c) a type of cake

4. Which sport does Bayern Munich play?
a) basketball
b) baseball
c) soccer

5. What is this?

Glossary

casket another name for a coffin

causeway raised path or road across water

composer person who writes music

coniferous describes a tree with needles instead of leaves that stays green all year round

emperor ruler of a group of countries, called an empire

inquisitive interested in learning about the world

maiden another name for a girl

Marco Polo explorer who lived from about 1254 to 1324. He traveled from Italy to China.

mudflat flat, muddy land that is covered by sea at high tide

parliament meeting of the rulers of a country

port place where ships are loaded and unloaded

wind turbine machine that turns wind power into electrical power

Find Out More

Books

Burgan, Michael. *Germany in Our World* (Countries in Our World). Mankato, Minn.: Smart Apple Media, 2012.

Colson, Mary. *Germany* (Countries Around the World). Chicago: Heinemann Library, 2012.

Web sites

Facthound offers a safe, fun way to find Internet sites related to this book. All of the sites on Facthound have been researched by our staff.

Here's all you do:

Visit www.facthound.com

Type in this code: 9781410979940

Index

Aachen 6

Bavaria 8, 26
Berlin 12, 28
Berlin Philharmonic
  Orchestra 23
Berlin Wall 7, 12
Black Forest 9
Black Forest gateau 21
Brandenburg Gate 12

car making 24
cathedrals 6, 19
Charlemagne 6
Christmas markets 18
cities 7, 12–13, 17, 28
Cologne Cathedral 19
currency 28

East Germany 7
Elbe River 13

food 18, 20–21
forests 9

Hamburg 13

islands 27

language 14, 28
Lorelei rock 10

map of Germany 5
Marco Polo 4, 30
mountains 8, 28
Munich 22
music 23

Neuschwanstein Castle
  26
North Frisian Islands 27
Nuremberg 18

population 15, 28
ports 13, 30

Reichstag 12
religion 19, 28
Rhine River 10, 28
rivers 10, 13, 28

schools 16
soccer 22
sports 22
Sylt 27

Wadden Sea National
  Park 11
West Germany 7
wildlife 11
wind farms 25

Zugspitze 8, 28